CW01560467

THE HIDDEN POWER OF
FORGIVENESS

BECOMING FREE FROM THE DEADLY ROOTS OF
BITTERNESS

JOSEPH NIPAH

authorHOUSE®

AuthorHouse™ UK Ltd.
1663 Liberty Drive
Bloomington, IN 47403 USA
www.authorhouse.co.uk
Phone: 0800.197.4150

© *2014 Joseph Nipah. All rights reserved.*

This is the second edition.

No part of this book may be reproduced, stored in a retrieval system, or transmitted by any means without the written permission of the author.

Published by AuthorHouse   10/13/2014

ISBN: 978-1-4969-8971-0 (sc)
ISBN: 978-1-4969-8972-7 (hc)
ISBN: 978-1-4969-8973-4 (e)

Any people depicted in stock imagery provided by Thinkstock are models, and such images are being used for illustrative purposes only.

Certain stock imagery © *Thinkstock.*

This book is printed on acid-free paper.

Because of the dynamic nature of the Internet, any web addresses or links contained in this book may have changed since publication and may no longer be valid. The views expressed in this work are solely those of the author and do not necessarily reflect the views of the publisher, and the publisher hereby disclaims any responsibility for them.

NIV

> *Scripture quotations marked NIV are taken from the Holy Bible, New International Version®. NIV®. Copyright* © *1973, 1978, 1984 by International Bible Society. Used by permission of* Zondervan*. All rights reserved. [*Biblica*]*

KJV

> *Scripture quotations marked KJV are from the Holy Bible, King James Version (Authorized Version). First published in 1611. Quoted from the KJV Classic Reference Bible, Copyright* © *1983 by The* Zondervan *Corporation.*

NKJV

> *Scripture quotations marked NKJV are taken from the New King James Version. Copyright* © *1982 by* Thomas Nelson, Inc*. Used by permission. All rights reserved.*

GNT

> *Scripture quotations marked GNT are taken from the Good News Translation — Second Edition. Copyright* © *1992 by* American Bible Society*. Used by permission. All rights reserved.*

DEDICATION

I dedicate this book to my dear wife Evelyn for her love and support through the difficult periods of our lives together. I am eternally grateful to God for allowing you to be part of my life. To my children Theophilus, Michelle and Kwame, who have had to endure extended periods of my absence from home in my professional and ministerial pursuits; I love you very much.

CONTENTS

ACKNOWLEDGEMENTS

One person who has been a great inspiration to me is Reverend Professor Osei Safo-Kantanka, whose commitment, balance and ingenuity stirred up gifts within me that I did not know I had. As a young undergraduate student working directly under his supervision, I observed him effectively managing and excelling in ministry, politics, academics, high administrative positions and family commitments with such balance and dexterity. As a result, I admitted to myself that I needed not shelve any gift in me before I could excel in another; it was possible to develop and excel in all of them. It was this conviction that gives me the energy to find time out of my very busy schedule to write and publish books to bless my generation. I also benefited from his perspective on the thoughts in this book. Prof, I am grateful to God for your life.

I am very grateful to Dr Ezekiel and Dr (Mrs.) Funmi Alawale, the Senior Pastors of God's Vineyard Ministries, UK. You have been of great inspiration to me. Your leadership, balance and prayer lives stir me up always. The effective ways in which you manage the high demands of medical practice, ministry and family commitments have left great impressions in my life. I am grateful to God for your lives.

I am also grateful to the entire leadership of God's Vineyard Ministries for the opportunity given me to serve in the Master's Vineyard. The immense support from the leadership and congregation of the Loughborough branch of the church is deeply appreciated. I derive great inspiration from the team day after day. I value your input in my life.

I also pay special tribute to Rev Dr Ebenezer Sefah; the General Overseer of Refreshing Hour International Church, whose drive and enthusiasm gave me the strength to carry on when I felt like giving up. I also thank Rev Daniel Karikari and Pastor Justice Arthur and my son Theophilus who helped with editing of the manuscript.

The wonderful support given me by my wife Evelyn is greatly appreciated. Finally, I would like to acknowledge the role of my children whose love and tenderness give so much meaning to my life. I pray for God to bless everyone who made this publication possible.

FOREWORD

There is a Ghanaian proverb, which literally translates; "The branches of trees that are close, inevitably rub against each other". The message of this proverb is that conflicts and hurts are unavoidable between people who are close to each other – friends, married couples, parents and their children, workmates, church and fellowship members, etc.

There is also another proverb which says; "To err is human and to forgive divine". This proverb also underlies the reality of conflicts and hurts and the need for us to rise beyond our ordinary humanity in order to handle our hurts and resolve our conflicts.

The Christian message is indeed about forgiveness. In his book, "The Contemporary Christian", John Stott describes our need for forgiveness in this story: "Not long before she died in 1988, in a moment of surprising candour on television, Marghanita Leski, one of our best-known secular humanists and novelists, said: 'What I envy most about you Christians is your forgiveness; I have nobody to forgive me'"

The problem of guilt is real. One of the consequences of sin is guilt. The Bible declares that *"All have sinned and fallen short of the glory of God" (Rom 3:23)*. This implies that; all are guilty before God, and this is real. The Christian, however, has the assurance that in Christ, God has forgiven them, their sins. Therefore, he/she can now shout; I am free from the guilt of sin!

Jesus taught us to pray; "Forgive us our sins as we forgive those who have sinned against us". Those who have been forgiven must learn to forgive. Therefore the ability to forgive (which is divine) is an important testimony that one's sins have been forgiven him/her by God.

In addition, when hurts are not dealt with, it leads to bitterness, which wears the body away like cancer and destroys all others around the bitter person. That is why I am happy that Dr. Joseph Nipah has taken on this important subject. What I find most helpful in this book is the fact that he illustrates the issue with a number of practical examples.

The story of how bitterness blocks the healing power of God and other graces from God is a classic example of how we can ruin our lives and cut ourselves from divine anointing and empowerment. The story of how Joseph handled his hurts and learned to forgive his brothers is classic and has been very well treated by the author.

Note that forgiving our neighbours is not a one-time event, since to err is human. You must not just read this book once and drop it, but read it any time you hurt someone and are made aware of it, or you are hurt by someone. Ask for God's grace to learn to forgive and it will bring health to your bones

Rt. Rev. Prof. Osei Safo-Kantanka
Bishop of Kumasi Diocese
Methodist Church, Ghana

THE ENCOUNTER

The issue of forgiveness is very difficult to deal with, and many who have experienced difficulties forgiving the wrongs others have caused them usually feel justified to remain bitter against the perpetrators of their pain and suffering. This realisation dawned on me many years ago as a young believer, in an encounter which left me very sad and made me reflect deeply on the teachings of Jesus on forgiveness. I was part of a team of young and dynamic Christians, whose short term vision was to reach the remote parts of Ghana, in the West Coast of Africa with the Word of God. It was our desire to demonstrate that Jesus Christ is the same yesterday, today and forever (*Heb 13:8*). A three day gospel crusade had been scheduled to take place in a village, and a team of about 12 people had come down to the venue ahead of the entire group in the afternoon of the first day of the crusade to prepare the grounds. Soon after we had entered the village, one of our hosts, who was a member of the group and the one who initiated the idea for the crusade, invited us to the house of a lady to pray for her sick son. When we entered the room, we were met with a sight that has never left my mind ever since. Right in the middle of the room and in front of a bed sat a boy with the stature of a seven to eight year old. He was sitting unsteadily on the floor with house flies all over him. The mother tried from time to time to drive off the flies. He was trembling from his waist upwards and could not coordinate his movements properly. I do not quite remember whether he could hear us, but he was foaming from the mouth and could not talk. He could not move about and depended completely on the mother's care. We were quite surprised when the mother revealed that he was 15 years of age and had been in that condition for over seven years. She explained with tears all over her face that her son was a very healthy, normal child till the age of seven; when he was stricken with the infirmity. He had since been deteriorating with the condition, and had hardly showed any further signs of growth.

This for us, however, was a great opportunity to demonstrate God's healing power, and to have an advantage of a living testimony on the opening night of the crusade; as it happened in *Acts 3:1 – 12; 4:4*, which led to an increase in the church to 5000 people in a single day. The sheer determination of the members of the team to witness the total deliverance of the lad was evident, with every one pacing around and praying in the Spirit even before we were given the green light to start praying. We shared the word of God briefly with the mother and joined our hands together to form a circle around the boy, and started praying earnestly in the Spirit and in understanding. We rebuked the evil powers behind the infirmity to lose their grip on the boy. While we were praying, the leader of the team commanded the boy to rise up as he held him by the hand. Suddenly, and to the great amazement of the mother, the boy leaped up to his feet smiling widely. Though he felt quite uneasy and was trembling from head to toe, he took his first step forward in over seven years. As you would imagine, the excitement was overwhelming. The mother in particular was dancing all around the room. The person supporting him to stand quickly stepped aside to allow the lad to move about on his own. Before long, he was pacing up and down the room with apparent excitement about what was happening.

With many of us filled with tears of joy, we kept up the prayers for complete deliverance, as his movement was still quite unsteady and he could yet not speak. However, in spite of the great faith and intense prayers, nothing more was happening. Just then the Lord gave us a revelation through a couple of the members of the team, indicating that there was a cause that needed to be dealt with before total deliverance could be possible. We could not really understand the full meaning of the messages; we therefore suspended the prayers and interviewed the mother about what really had happened. It was then that she revealed her deep bitterness against a sister whom she believed was the cause of the boy's predicament. She told a sad story of how she lost her husband the same year the boy came down with the disease. She linked these incidences to some happenings that made her believe that the sister was the spiritual brain behind all her sufferings. While weeping uncontrollably, she revealed that if she ever had the chance, she would not hesitate to end the life of the sister, in order to inflict similar pain to her family. Following this realisation, we attempted to take her through the teachings of Jesus on forgiveness. We made her clearly aware that if she could let go of her bitterness, the Lord was going to complete the healing, which we had all dramatically witnessed unfolding before our own eyes. Knowing how hard she was struggling with what the Lord was requesting of her, we spent a great amount of time trying to convince her to carefully consider the issue at stake. We pleaded that if not for herself, she should let go of her pain for the sake of her son; because God had clearly revealed that it was the key to his total deliverance.

Her final words broke my heart and erased every conviction I had sustained for the boy's complete healing. She told us in plain words that if she gave any of us the impression that she could ever forgive her sister in her lifetime, it would be a lie; she knew deep within her heart that she could never bring herself to do that. We did not know how to proceed from there, and so sadly, this great miracle that had started unfolding so beautifully before our very eyes, had to end just there. We simply prayed for God's mercy and left the house with great disappointment. I never heard anything about that boy again, but that encounter made me realise how difficult it is sometimes to forgive, even when the benefits are clear to us.

I may never know how much pain you are carrying in your heart, or whatever the reason is that made you decide to read this book. There is one thing, however, that I can assure you of: as I write these pages, I am praying, and will continue to pray for everyone who will read this book. Many of us need special grace to be able to deal with the painful wounds of our past. It is my prayer that the Lord will pour this grace upon you to have the willingness and the ability to let go of that which may have denied you of the peace God intended for you.

> *"For it is God which worketh in you both to will and to do of His good pleasure"*
> **(Phil 2:13 KJV)**

CHAPTER 1

DEAL WITH YOUR HURT BEFORE IT SINKS YOU INTO BITTERNESS

Through experiences such as the encounter such as the afore mentioned encounter with the youngster, the Lord has taught me to clearly understand that it does not take only covenants with mediums, fetishes or ancestral spirits to experience demonic invasion and resistance from the Devil. Living in disobedience to God for instance, could empower the enemy to resist the authority that Jesus has delegated to us as Christians. It is very important for believers to understand that we are engaged in very real spiritual warfare; which is guided by spiritual principles. *"For though we walk in the flesh, we do not war after the flesh"* (*2Cor 10:3 KJV*). It is equally important to note that the weapons at our disposal in this warfare are undeniably effective in pulling down every stronghold of the Devil (*2Cor 10:4-5*). However, there is a very important condition for effective use of these weapons to deal with the Devil's resistance in any situation of life. **You must be under authority to command authority**. If you are having serious trouble dealing with what is clearly an operation of the Devil, one of the questions you may need to ask yourself is whether you are walking in obedience to God.

One tool the Devil uses to deny Christians the full enjoyment of our inheritance is bitterness. Bitterness is subtle, but very deadly. It does not just happen, but results from unresolved hurts. Every normal human being is subject to the emotion of hurt; everyone feels hurt when not treated well. That is to say everyone has been hurt at one time or another. To hurt someone is to cause pain to the person's feelings. For example, when someone treats you with disrespect or shouts at you in public; you are likely to experience an unpleasant feeling. That is *'hurt'*. It is absolutely normal to feel that way. In all forms of relationships, whether casual or serious friendships, platonic or intimate, we are bound to hurt one another through our actions. Even well intended actions could cause pain to other people's feelings, due to the complexities of human nature and natural limitations. 'Hurt' may result from misunderstanding each other or misinterpreting each other's actions.

An instance is the case of a young Christian Brother, John who was interested in Fiona *(not their real names)*, a member of their fellowship group. One day John was seeing Fiona off after a fellowship meeting, in the company of another brother, George. When they arrived at the entrance of Fiona's residence, while intending to bid them both goodbye, Fiona said 'thanks George; see you tomorrow.' At that point, John experienced an unpleasant feeling in his heart. He felt ignored, rejected and quite hurt. Addressing George alone and not both of them made him feel embarrassingly irrelevant. It instantly sent him a signal that Fiona had no interest in him at all. The hurt and the pain resulting from what John considered to be a rejection by Fiona lasted quite a while. It later turned out that Fiona had no such intentions; she was not even aware that something had gone so badly wrong that evening.

I also read about another incident that caused a lady to bear much pain in her heart for many years against her father. She and her sister were brought up by their biological parents in an atmosphere of love and affection until something happened that changed her disposition in a negative way. One day, she opened their father's wallet to find a passport picture of her sister nicely displayed in one of the transparent pockets of the wallet. She was fascinated by the idea of having their pictures displayed in their dad's wallet. She thought that the reason her picture was not displayed was because her dad did not have a copy of hers. She therefore slotted one of her pictures which she most admired in the wallet next to her sister's without telling their father. After sometime, when she took her dad's wallet, to her utter disappointment, her sister's picture was intact, but hers was not in place. She was obviously hurt and concluded then that she was not loved.

What I could not quite understand as I read that story was why she did not ask for an explanation from her dad. It could have made all the difference. So many people carry hurtful feelings in their hearts against loved ones, friends, members of their families, churches, pastors, corporate bodies, etc, due to unfulfilled or disappointed expectations; but they fail to do anything about their feelings. On many occasions, relationships could have been saved from irreparable consequences of unresolved hurts, if only steps had been taken in time to address the issues that brought about the hurtful feelings.

To help the reader gain a better understanding of why this is so, let me explain how hurts that may appear harmless from the beginning, could progress into a state that could destroy any relationship.

1. ANGER, HURT AND BITTERNESS

To have a strong feeling about something or to be hurt by another's action may not be wrong, but how you handle such harmless feelings is extremely important. We are emotional beings; God created us that way. Regarding the emotion of anger for instance, *Eph 4:26* states, '*be ye angry---*'. Jesus himself was angry when his Father's house of prayer was turned into a den of thieves (*Matt 21:13*). It is therefore important for us to understand that expressing such natural emotions in response to someone's actions towards you may not necessarily be the problem. Rather it is how we manage it that may be the issue. *Eph 4:26 (KJV)* which states, '*be ye angry*', concludes with a caution, '*and sin not, let not the sun go down upon your wrath.'* As harmless as the feeling of hurt may be, if it is not handled well, it sinks the individual harbouring that feeling into a deeper state – the state of bitterness – which becomes a stronghold.

2. THE DESTRUCTIVE POWER OF BITTERNESS

To explain the destructive power of bitterness, let us pay careful attention to the underlined portions of *Heb 12:15.*

> **"Looking diligently, <u>lest any man fail of the grace of God</u>; lest any <u>root of bitterness</u> springing up <u>trouble you,</u> and thereby <u>many be defiled</u> (Heb 12:15 KJV)."**

a. Bitterness could cause you to miss the grace of God

The expression "*<u>Looking diligently lest any man fail of the grace of God</u>*" emphasises the need to be careful so that no one misses or loses the grace of God. In other versions of scripture, the word *'fail'* is translated *'miss'* or *'fall short'.* Whichever way you look at it, the implication is for us to be careful so that the grace of God does not get *'out of our reach'.* Many Christians only associate God's grace with salvation. Indeed, it is only by grace that any of us can consider ourselves qualified for heaven; but there is more to grace than that. It represents divine backing. God's grace can bestow special abilities upon an individual to succeed under challenging circumstances. Grace makes you able to do or achieve what your own strength cannot achieve. It could give you favour before men. Joseph experienced this favour while he was in slavery and in prison, as recorded in *Gen 39:1-5, 22-23*. When Joseph was brought down to Egypt as a slave, and also when he subsequently became a prisoner; The LORD was said to be with him and He made everything Joseph did to be successful.

Much more, even where there is no favour but rejection; the grace of God could still enable you to produce results that even your opponents cannot ignore, just as Peter and John. They were described as uneducated ordinary men by the Jewish leaders. However, the difference Jesus had made in their lives and the evidence resulting from the grace God had bestowed upon their lives and ministry amazed the leaders *(Acts 4:13)*. We simply cannot do without the grace of God.

Does it not scare you then to note that a believer could miss or fail to access the grace of God? I admonish you therefore to maintain a disposition that will enable you to deal promptly and decisively with anything that could threaten the grace of God upon your life. This is one important reason why you should not allow your hurts to sink you down into bitterness.

b. Bitterness is likened to a root (usually hidden)

The writer of Hebrews refers to *the root of bitterness* as a state which could deny a believer of such divine presence. Roots are generally hidden in the dark chambers of the soil. They slowly grow downwards, deeper and deeper until they soon become established. Bitterness is likened to a root; you may not see it, but it could be growing deeper and establishing itself with the passage of time. The longer this is allowed to go on, the more difficult it becomes to uproot it. With some types of plants, such as grasses, once their roots have been established; it becomes extremely difficult to eliminate them. Cutting off the shoots to the ground level, or even burning the leaves may only give temporary relief. All that is needed is for the rain to pour down and sink into the soil to make the right nutrients available to the roots, and shoots quickly *spring up* again. To eliminate it permanently, you must deal with the roots.

Many people who are having problems relating with others simply try to deal with issues that spring out of the *root of bitterness*. The truth is, until the issues involved are rooted out or opened up and dealt with, there will always be issues to deal with. Issues that otherwise would not have become sources of conflicts, could easily become serious bones of contention, because of the fuel being injected by roots of bitterness that have been covered.

c. Bitterness will invariably trouble you

The dangers of bitterness, however, go beyond its root-like nature. If roots of bitterness are allowed to develop unresolved, the sort of things which would spring up out of them could be devastating.

Heb 12:15 emphasises further that the undesirable effects of the roots of bitterness, could *trouble you,* the embittered person. Nurturing bitter feelings against someone, irrespective of the causes, do have negative consequences. A bitter person could succeed in masking his or her feelings and feign affection towards the object of their bitterness, but with the passage of time the symptoms become clearly evident. Masked and suppressed ill-feelings, or ignored hurts mature and find outlets of expression. Making continued effort to suppress bitter feelings will only make you a hypocrite.

Since unresolved hurts develop into bitterness, it is prudent to prevent bitterness by dealing promptly with things that hurt you; especially those you cannot simply ignore. Let me clarify here though that I do not mean to ask you to make a case out of every little issue and convene formal sessions for resolution. No, not at all! Certainly it is not every issue that must be taken to heart. There will be issues you will simply have to ignore. In fact, that is a mark of maturity. Love indeed covers a multitude of sins *(1Pet 4:8).* It is a sign of immaturity in relationships to be upset about every little thing. Such an attitude makes people too cautious in relating with you because they would not want to hurt you. Such an attitude will only make you lose friends. Having said that however, there are issues or situations where the best way out will be not to allow sleeping dogs to lie. Once you are genuinely hurt about an issue, which you can not simply forget or trivialise, you need to address it the proper way.

Absalom's failure to deal with his hurt and its consequences:

An example is an incident that is recorded in *2Sam 13*. During the reign of David as the King of Israel, an appalling incident happened in his household. However, those who were directly affected by this despicable act failed to confront the issue with the seriousness it required. This eventually led to devastating consequences for the entire household.

In the course of time, Amnon son of David fell in love with Tamar, the beautiful sister of Absalom son of David. Amnon became so obsessed with his sister Tamar that he made himself ill. She was a virgin, and it seemed impossible for him to do anything to her... So Amnon lay down and pretended to be ill.

When the king came to see him, Amnon said to him, "I would like my sister Tamar to come and make some special bread in my sight, so I may eat from her hand." David sent word to Tamar at the palace: ... And Tamar took the bread she had prepared and brought it to her brother Amnon in his bedroom. But when she took it to him to eat, he grabbed her ... **and since he was stronger than she, he raped her.** *Then Amnon ... said to her, Get up and get out! "No"! she said to him. "Sending me away would be a greater wrong than what you have already done to me". But ... his servant put her out and bolted the door after her. She was wearing an ornate robe, for this was the kind of garment the virgin daughters of the king wore. Tamar put ashes on her head and tore the ornate robe she was wearing. Her brother Absalom said to her,* **"Has that Amnon, your brother, been with you? Be quiet for now, my sister; he is your brother. Don't take this thing to heart."** *And Tamar lived in her brother Absalom's house, a desolate woman. When King David heard all this, he was furious.* **Absalom never said a word to Amnon, either good or bad**; *he hated Amnon because he had disgraced his sister Tamar.*

(2Sam 13:1–22 NIV)

Considering the circumstances surrounding this disgraceful act by Amnon, you are likely to agree with me that this was by no means an issue for Absalom to play down on as he appeared to have done. In my counselling experiences, I have come across situations which ended up explosively because victims were advised to forget about issues they should have been encouraged to discuss. Absalom advised her grieving sister *"Be quiet now, my sister; he is your brother. Don't take this thing to heart"*; and this may be quite familiar to some readers. For several reasons including fear, desire for peaceful coexistence, efforts to preserve family reputation or dignity of individuals in respectable positions in society, or by virtue of the sensitive nature of some issues; sometimes what should be brought to the fore and treated are rather shrouded in secrecy.

Bishop T. D Jakes, the renowned American preacher was correct in saying 'things that are covered don't heal well.' The reason why roots of bitterness that are allowed to spring up tend to *"trouble you"* is that covered emotional wounds do not heal; rather they create complications. As *'Tamar lived in her brother Absalom's house, a desolate woman'*, what the world around them thought had been forgotten was actually growing and taking deep roots in Absalom. When their father David heard of the incident, though he expressed his anger, he failed to deal appropriately with it. Absalom on his part hated what Amnon had done to Tamar, but he *never said a word to Amnon, either good or bad,* until after two whole years - - -

***Two years later**, when Absalom's sheepshearers were at Baal Hazor near the border of Ephraim, he invited all the king's sons to come there. Absalom went to the king and said, "Your servant has had shearers come. Will the king and his attendants please join me?" "No, my son," the king replied. "All of us should not go; we would only be a burden to you." Although Absalom urged him, he still refused to go but gave him his blessing. Then Absalom said, "If not, please let my brother Amnon come with us." The king asked him, "Why should he go with you?" But Absalom urged him, so he sent with him Amnon and the rest of the king's sons. **Absalom ordered his men, "Listen! When Amnon is in high spirits from drinking wine and I say to you, 'Strike Amnon down,' then kill him.** Don't be afraid. Haven't I given you this order? Be strong and brave." **So Absalom's men did to Amnon what Absalom had ordered**. Then all the king's sons got up, mounted their mules and fled.*
(2Sam 13:23–29 NIV)

It is said that time is a healer, but experience has taught me otherwise when it comes to dealing with bitterness. The passage of time does not erase unresolved hurts which were not forgiven. After two whole years, the true intentions of Absalom became evident when he plotted a scheme to vent his spleen on Amnon. He subsequently killed him in broad daylight. This resulted in a series of disastrous consequences for David's family. In the end, Absalom himself lost his life under tragic circumstances.

Beloved, bitterness does not only have damaging implications for whoever you may consider as the cause of your pain, it has similar implications for the embittered person as well.

The offspring of the roots of bitterness will "*trouble you*" because a state of bitterness is **a state of unforgiveness**, which is **a state of sin.** These conditions could obviously give the Devil room to operate against the believer, or to resist the authority we have in Christ. The Apostle Paul understood this truth to the core, and therefore admonished that we should forgive "*Lest Satan should get an advantage of us: for we are not ignorant of his devices*" (*2Cor 2:11 KJV*). From the day King Saul started harbouring bitterness in his heart against David, evil spirits began to trouble him. Beloved reader, consider these truths carefully. There is nothing to gain by remaining in a state of bitterness; it will only make you a loser.

> "*And Saul was very wroth, and the saying displeased him; and he said, They have*

ascribed unto David ten thousands, and to me they have ascribed but thousands: and what can he have more but the kingdom? And Saul eyed David from that day and forward. And it came to pass on the morrow, that the evil spirit from God came upon Saul, and he prophesied in the midst of the house: and David played with his hand, as at other times: and there was a javelin in Saul's hand. And Saul cast the javelin; for he said, I will smite David even to the wall with it. And David avoided out of his presence twice."
(1Sam 18: 8-11 KJV)

d. Your bitterness affects other people around you

Finally, *Hebrews 12:15* concludes by emphasising the effects of bitterness on others "- - - *and thereby many be defiled*". Bitterness does not only trouble you; it affects other people around you who may have nothing to do whatsoever with your pain. Let me explain how this happens by drawing your attention to some symptoms of bitterness. Many people harbouring bitterness in their hearts live in denial. When confronted with the truth about their negative emotions, they may defend that they have no ill-feelings towards the object of their bitterness. There are, however, certain manifestations that could indicate the true state of a heart filled with bitterness. When people become bitter, their perspective about the object of their bitterness is altered in such a way that it becomes difficult to appreciate anything about that individual.

To help you assess your heart in order to ascertain if you are harbouring bitterness against anyone, ask yourself the following questions:

- When others are excited about the life, exploits, performances or achievements of an individual, do you easily find reasons to downplay the achievements of this person?
- Do you feel uncomfortable when other people begin to sing the praises of the person you have such issues with?
- Do you find it difficult to initiate positive conversations with other people about this individual?
- Rather, are you more inclined to contribute toward discussions that focus on the failings or negatives in that person?

If you answered 'yes' to any of these questions, it may be indicative of the root of bitterness taking its roots in your heart. The more you answered yes to these questions, the more the likelihood that you are dealing with bitterness.

An important observation to make about these questions, which are designed to help us diagnose or acknowledge the presence of bitterness in one's heart, is that they all involve conversations or interaction with other people. This is why "*thereby* [or as a result of bitterness] *many* [will] *be defiled.*" To defile something is to corrupt, ruin or pollute it. Bitter people have the tendency to pollute the minds of others around them against the person they have issues with. Indeed it is dangerous to hang around persons with bitterness in their hearts. They have tremendous power to alter your positive perception about the person who is the cause of their pain.

For example in a church setting; sometimes people feel disappointed in the leadership, the pastor or the way things are done. But they fail to handle their hurts appropriately. As a result, their hurt is allowed to sink them into a state of bitterness. In this state, they stop focusing on any good thing happening in the church. Such people have the tendency to mess up the commitment of even new comers, who may be oblivious of any misgivings. It is sad to say that many break ups in churches today are not engineered by divine purpose, but originate rather from unresolved bitter disputes. Bitterness has been an effective divisive tool in the hands of the devil against many relationships. Do not be ignorant of his devices; prevent it by dealing appropriately with your hurts.

> *See to it that no one falls short of the grace of God and that no bitter root grows up to cause trouble and defile many* **(Heb 12:15 NIV)**

CHAPTER 2

ESCAPE THE BITTERNESS TRAP

1. ACCEPT THAT THERE IS BITTERNESS IN YOUR HEART

The very first step in overcoming any challenge in life is to acknowledge the situation. Failing to accept that there is an issue or a problem to be addressed will simply lead to complacency. In such a state, little or no effort is made to make the situation better. Let me illustrate this with a situation I had to deal with some time ago. I had a very pathetic encounter with a respected married man and a father of three lovely children, whom I observed to be slowly developing a mental illness. The reality of his mental condition soon became apparent to his close friends and relatives. With each passing day or week, we realised that he became more and more incoherent in his conversations and untidy in appearance. The wife became obviously very worried and confided in a group of friends of the husband's; of whom I was a part. The major problem she had with him was that he was refusing to accept that he had a problem, and therefore had refused any form of assistance. Truly, when we tried to convince him to cooperate with the family to see a psychiatrist and also to be prayed for, he did not take kindly to the implications of our request. Finally, when things really got out of hand and they succeeded in getting him to see a doctor, he refused to take his medication. He still insisted, even then, that as far as he was concerned, there was nothing wrong with him. As you would imagine, this man could not be helped. And it was mainly because he was living in denial.

In the same way, as long as a person harbouring bitterness refuses to accept that reality, very little could be done to help the situation. Having realised how damaging bitterness could be for you as a Christian, it will be in your interest to own up to any traces of bitterness in your heart. This will pave the way to receiving the right prescription for your total healing. Scripture admonishes in 2Cor 13:5 *(KJV)*, *"Examine yourselves, whether ye be in the faith; prove your own selves."* Signs and symptoms are usually the first observations a doctor would examine to diagnose the type of disease a patient may be suffering from. I encourage you to critically and honestly examine yourself in the same manner regarding your present and past relationships. It will guide you in determining whether you are truly free from the symptoms of bitterness as explained in the previous chapter.

2. DO NOT TAKE THE ISSUE OF FORGIVENESS LIGHTLY

The next important reason why many have been trapped in the deep roots of bitterness is that they take the issue of forgiveness lightly. From experience and on the basis of scriptural evidence, I am fully persuaded that forgiveness is the way out of bitterness. Nonetheless, I am also convinced that, to be able to attack deeply rooted resentments and successfully deal with them, one should **never take forgiveness for granted**. Trivialising the issue of forgiveness could be likened to attempting to lift a very heavy load, which you had underestimated as a light-weighted object. You are most likely to hurt your back. Your posture, fortitude, approach and general attitude in the attempt to lift that load, would be determined by your assessment of its weight. Approaching issues regarding forgiveness in a casual or trivial manner could easily cause more hurt. You should always remember that there is a strong man behind the scenes; the Devil, who is determined to keep you in the bonds of bitterness. He does this in order to deny you the three-fold gift of peace; with which the Spirit of God has blessed the believer – peace _with God_, the peace _of God_ and peace _with men_.

Through personal experiences and lessons I continue to learn in my encounters with people, particularly through counselling experiences, I have come to conclude that the pathway of forgiveness is not an easy way. For anyone to succeed in reaching the end of that pathway, particularly in dealing with issues that have resulted in deep emotional wounds, it is necessary to first acknowledge that it is not an easy choice. As I wrote these pages, I was reminded of the struggles a young lady went through in her attempt to heed my advice to forgive her father. He had caused her a great deal of hurt and was still causing a lot of pain to the entire family. Some days after a counselling session with her, she handed me an 18–page note and said to me 'Pastor, I am not mad, I am not insane, I only wanted to express my struggles as truly as I felt'. This is how it began:

> *"Dear God, this is how I truly feel. I believe I can express myself better on paper than in speech."*

She then went ahead to give a heart moving account of the confusion and the struggles she was experiencing; as she made the effort to accept the truth being presented to her from the word of God, and her difficulties in dealing with the persistent pain being caused by the father's attitude. Portions of her note read:

> **"I know I have been asked to make a quality decision to forgive once and for all. With time, the scars may fade away and I'll let go – but I've got nothing against Daddy. I feel sorry**

for him. But I cannot lie that I will not be hurt or annoyed by what he constantly does. This is why it troubles me to know whether I have forgiven or not." - - - "Sometimes when I find myself thinking a certain way or doing some things he does, I hate myself so much. I hate myself because I believe I'm not supposed to be like that; and still wonder – if I'm really born again, why am I struggling in my thought realm or actions?"

This is a typical example of the dilemma many go through when confronted with the issue of forgiveness. Considering such experiences, and indeed my personal struggles in dealing with issues of bitterness in my own life, it would be irresponsible on my part to simply say forgiveness is the way out; without giving compelling reasons why it is so.

3. CONSIDER WHAT YOU LOSE FOR REMAINING IN BITTERNESS

Why then should every serious minded Christian make every effort to forgive the misdeeds of others and live at peace with all men in spite of the apparent practical difficulties involved?

a. Choosing to remain in bitterness is a choice to remain a loser.

The problem with the sin of unforgiveness is that it is an on-going condition of darkness in the heart, a place where the love of God is supposed to spring from. Just as light and darkness can not dwell together, so does a heart filled with bitterness find difficulty in reaching the presence of God. While I was working on the original manuscript of this book, the Lord impressed upon our hearts to declare three days of fasting and prayers in the church where I was serving as a pastor. Our obedience to this call resulted in one of the greatest moves of God I have ever observed or experienced. In our prayers, we followed two main leadings of the Spirit; to avert some evil that appeared to be looming over the congregation and to overcome every impediment in our lives which could prevent us from receiving what the Lord had released for us to enjoy. On the third day, we organised an all-night prayer vigil to crown the programme. And what an awesome worship experience we had that night! Several people came under tremendous influence of the Holy Spirit. Some fell down completely helpless, while others went into what appeared to be a deep sleep. At the end of the session, some of the people shared their experiences of what had happened to them while they were under the influence of the Holy Spirit. Among the testimonies, two were of particular significance to me; they related very much with the truth the Lord had impressed on my heart to write about in this book. Both messages emphasised the need for many of us in the service to deal with bitterness in our hearts to pave the way to receive the blessings God had made available to us. One of them explained her experience in the following words: *"I saw the Lord distributing gifts to several individuals, but he ignored some people, passing by them to give to others. When he got to my turn, he passed on without looking at me. I became very worried and wondered why the Lord could ignore me at such a crucial moment; having committed myself wholeheartedly to the entire three days of fasting and prayer programme. Then the Lord then turned and said to me that my heart was not ready for his gift, because it was filled with so much unforgiveness and bitterness".* You can imagine how I felt as I sat there listening to this lady who had no idea of what the Lord was impressing on my heart as I wrote the thoughts in this book. This explains why God in his wisdom directed that:

> *Therefore, if you are offering your gift at the altar and there remember that your brother or sister has something against you, leave your gift there in front of the altar. First go and be reconciled to them; then come and offer your gift.* **(Matt 5:23, 24 NIV)**

Why? Quite clearly, you will be wasting your precious time and resources if you go ahead with your worship; it cannot reach God's awesome presence. It breaks my heart to observe time and time again, precious children of God going through issues and crying out to God with no results. I need to say that though this does not always imply divine disapproval; in certain instances it is the reason for the loss of divine presence.

Some time ago, our church had a revival meeting with a servant of God, who is the Pastor of a vibrant church in the capital city of Ghana, Accra and also a successful business man. In one of the meetings, he narrated a bitter experience he had in his business career. Before he became a pastor, he worked as a sales representative in a pharmaceutical shop. After some time, he uncovered some corrupt practices in the organisation, which he could not be party to. After making his position quite clear to the manager, he decided to resign.

A couple of days after he submitted his resignation letter to the secretary, he received a rather shocking reaction from the manager. In a letter dated a few days before the date on his letter of resignation, the manager had dismissed him from the company for no apparent reason. He later learnt from the secretary that the manager asked her to write the dismissal letter after receiving his notice of resignation, and asked her to backdate it in order to nullify his resignation. This was designed to prevent him from receiving any entitlements from the company.

These developments made him very angry and bitter, but he was in no position to challenge this injustice. From this point on, regardless of how much he prayed and waited upon the Lord, his situation deteriorated from bad to worse. He remained unemployed for a whole year. During this period, he became increasingly bitter and wished he could find a way to pay back the manager in his own coin. While he was in this state of confusion, the Lord dealt with him one evening during a revival meeting. He received a direct message from the Lord, asking him how long he wanted to delay his blessings by harbouring bitterness in his heart. That evening, he broke down in tears before God. He confessed all the deep pains in his heart and asked for forgiveness and the grace to forgive his former manager. Soon after this encounter, his life turned around in a dramatic way. He did not simply get a job; he registered his own pharmaceutical company through a miraculous contact that God brought in his way. I personally believe that this open door had been put in place by God moments after he was so cruelly treated by his former employer. However, he could not appropriate it because of the barrier of bitterness in his heart.

Such experiences have made it quite apparent to me that many of us have wasted days, weeks and months of fasting and waiting on the Lord, because the channels through which He will release the blessings we are calling Him for, are clogged with bitterness. Indeed, it is not really the number of days of fasting you can pride yourself in that matters; it is how ready you are to receive the results when they are given.

b. Bitterness could deprive you of God's forgiveness

At a very young age of about seven years, I had been on holidays at my maternal grandfather's place. He was an Anglican priest. One afternoon, I had followed him to the church premises to have enough space to run around while he engaged a young lady in a counselling session. At one moment, when I came close to where they were having the discussion, I heard grandpa ask the lady; "have you ever thought seriously about the implications of the Lord's Prayer?" He then asked her to recite the prayer, which she did without difficulty. When she got to the part that says; *"and forgive us our trespasses as we forgive those who trespass against us",* he stopped her and asked her to repeat that a number of times. Though I knew the whole of the Lord's Prayer and could recite it without hesitation, as grandpa expatiated on the implications of this part of the prayer to the young lady, the truth dawned on my tender heart for the very first time.

> *And forgive us our debts, as we forgive our debtors. And lead us not into temptation, but deliver us from evil: For thine is the kingdom, and the power, and the glory, for ever. Amen. For if ye forgive men their trespasses, your heavenly Father will also forgive you: But if ye forgive not men their trespasses, neither will your Father forgive your trespasses.*
> **(Matt 6:12-15 KJV)**

And when ye stand praying, forgive, if ye have ought against any: that your Father also which is in heaven may forgive you your trespasses. But if ye do not forgive, neither will your Father which is in heaven forgive your trespasses.
(Mark 11:25, 26 KJV)

Many Christians do not give any serious thought to the words in these passages. Whenever we recite the Lord's Prayer, we reiterate this serious condition regarding how God should deal with us if we miss the mark. What we are saying in effect is that God's measure of forgiveness for us should be at the same level as we forgive others. So if we are only able to tolerate a couple of offences, we are asking the Lord to tolerate our misdeeds only a couple of times, and then deal mercilessly with us if we persist in it. A full understanding of this truth will help you stop at nothing in guarding your heart with diligence from any trace of bitterness or unforgiveness. Jesus further stressed the importance of this issue when he taught his disciples to take the initiative towards peace, restoration and forgiveness even when they were at the receiving end of offences (*Matt 18:15-17*). This obviously was more than they could bear, and Peter wondered how many times Jesus expected a hot tempered individual of his kind to forgive an offender. When Peter tried to restrict Jesus to numbers, he received the shock of his life with the answer Jesus gave.

> *Then came Peter to him, and said, Lord, how*
> *oft shall my brother sin against me, and I*
> *forgive him? Till seven times? Jesus saith unto*
> *him, I say not unto thee, Until seven times:*
> *but, Until seventy times seven.*
> **(Matt 18:21, 22 KJV)**

In response to the apparent surprised reaction of the disciples, Jesus went a step further. He told them the following parable to break down this hard truth, to allow them relate with it practically. A servant owed his master a lot of money and was not in a position to repay. According to the Life Application Bible commentary, the ten thousand talents owed by the servant amounted to millions of dollars. Therefore, the master ordered that his whole family and possessions be sold to defray some of the debt. When he fell on his knees, begging for more time, his master forgave him all the debt. He then stepped out and met a fellow servant who owed him very little amount of money; calculated to be only a few dollars. When he requested for his money, his colleague also fell on his knees begging him for time. However, to the shock of those who witnessed the situation, he refused to listen to the plea of his fellow servant and harassed him for his money. Those who saw what was happening reported back to the master (*Matt 18: 23-30*).

> *Then the master called the servant in. 'You*
> *wicked servant,' he said, 'I cancelled all that*
> *debt of yours because you begged me to.*

*Shouldn't you have had mercy on your fellow
servant just as I had on you?' In anger his
master handed him over to the jailers to be
tortured, until he should pay back all he owed.*
**"This is how my heavenly Father will treat
each of you unless you forgive your brother
or sister from your heart.**
(Matt 18: 31-35 NIV)

I had read this parable many times, but I had never really
thought of its implications until the day the Lord drew my
attention to the last verse. The last sentence was actually
Christ's application of the parable. As the true implication
of the parable dawned on me, my understanding of the
Bible's teachings on forgiveness was greatly challenged. I
asked myself whether Jesus really implied that our inability
to let go of the "*little*" sins others commit against us could
cause God to reconsider or hold us responsible for sins he
had already forgiven us? As I meditated deeply on this
realisation, I concluded that there should be no misdeed
committed against the believer that should be considered
as being beyond pardon. Compared to the sins we have
committed, and still commit against God; what others do
to us are indeed "*little*", and we should be able to let go.
God knows hurt, and we hurt Him all the time. The truth
however is, if God is asking us to forgive until seventy
times seven, you can be sure that He will hold no sin against
us for which we have repented, confessed and asked for His
forgiveness.

c. Bitterness gives the Devil a foothold in your life.

Even when it appears unreasonable to consider forgiving the wrongs someone has committed against you, it is still worth keeping the pathway of forgiveness open as much as it depends on you. This is because remaining in a state of unforgiveness could open a door for the Devil to gain access into your life.

> *"And do not give the devil a foothold...Get rid of all bitterness, rage and anger, brawling and slander, along with every form of malice. Be kind and compassionate to one another, forgiving each other, just as in Christ God forgave you".*
> **(Eph 4: 27, 31-32 NIV)**

Scripture refers to the Devil as a strong man who seeks to forcibly appropriate the portion of the believer as his own *(Matt 12:29)*. It is important for us to note that the strength of the natural man by itself cannot stand the Devil's strength. It takes a stronger man to overpower the enemy of the righteous and force him to let go of whatever he has wrongfully appropriated from us. Thank God! There is a stronger man; Jesus!! At the mention of His name, every knee must bow *(Luke 11:21-22)*. As believers, we have been given the authority to confront the powers of the Devil and destroy his influence over our lives. Through faith in the name of Jesus, the believer can cause the evil kingdom of the Devil to tremble. However, some things in the life of the believer could give the Devil some legal grounds to hold on. Bitterness is a typical example of such situations. That is why Scripture advises us to get rid of all bitterness and forgive one another in order not to give any foothold to the Devil. I have witnessed situations where Christians move from place to place, time after time in pursuit of deliverance. They pursued men of God for deliverance from one problem or another, but to no avail. That is not to say that the persistence of a problem in a believer's life indicates that the person is doing something wrong. No! That is not the message I am trying to pass across. Indeed, God responds to our requests in different ways; His answer may be yes, wait or no. However, when a Christian persistently goes through afflictions; it is advisable to re-examine one's life to determine whether there could be any identifiable underlying causes. The Devil does not have the capacity to resist the authority of Jesus' name which is released in faith by a righteous man; unless there is something wrong with the foundation of the righteous. *"If the foundations be destroyed, what can the righteous do? (Psalm 11:3 KJV)"* Check the foundations and mend any cracks you may identify. Free your heart from bitterness and enjoy the fullness of His grace.

4. REFUSE TO BE IMPRISONED BY YOUR PAST

Anyone who has ever been deeply hurt, especially by someone who is in a close and continuing relationship, knows how difficult it is to deal with it. It becomes even more difficult to deal with such hurts when it leaves long term effects or it results in a permanent misfortune. That could serve as a constant reminder of the experience. People in such situations may not see any wisdom in forgiving their offenders. They are likely to excuse their actions and convince themselves that anyone in their situation would feel and act the same way.

On one occasion, I was sharing some of the thoughts in this book on a morning devotional programme on a local radio station. A lady who claimed to be a Christian called into the programme during the phone-in session. She narrated how she gave her love and great support to a man she trusted who had promised to marry her. However, when this young man suddenly found himself in a prestigious position in life, he forgot about her and went off with another woman. This was obviously a devastating experience for the young lady. In her grief, she found a Muslim young man who appeared to fill up the vacuum left in her life so perfectly. She claimed the man showed her love and the support she needed during those vulnerable moments. She therefore did not hesitate when he asked her to marry him. It was only after the marriage that the full realisation of what she had gotten herself into became apparent to her. She had been persuaded to convert into a religion she hardly knew anything about. Besides, she had been married as the second wife to an overly abusive husband. She had become so despondent about life and had even contemplated suicide at one point. As you may imagine, she put the blame squarely on the former fiancé who disappointed her. She gave a clear indication of her deep bitterness against him. She revealed further that anytime she had to endure such pain, humiliation and unhappiness in life, as a result of her marital status, she became so resentful and wished that some terrible disaster would befall her former fiancé and his new found wife, wherever they may be.

While listening to her, I perceived that should this young lady know where that former fiancé lived, she most likely would have attempted to destroy him in any way possible. That certainly would have further complicated the issues she already had to deal with. In responding to her situation, I drew her attention to the real possibility of her never setting an eye on that man till the day she will die. For that reason, it was not in her interest to aggravate her pain by choosing to remain bitter against him. By maintaining that disposition, she has made a choice to permit the person to continue controlling her life, feelings, emotions, actions and so on for as long as she lives. I assured her of my understanding, sympathy, and total condemnation of the insensitivity of the former fiancé. However, to help put her on the pathway of recovery, which in my view was very possible; I realised that she had to be made to look at the situation from another perspective. I drew her attention to her own mistakes and the need to accept responsibility for her indiscretion, which would help her to seek help in dealing with the situation.

That may sound harsh to someone who may have gone through similar experiences. Like this lady, I have noted that many people allow past misfortunes to control their future. This situation tends to limit such people from appropriating the opportunities the Lord brings their way. My conviction is that **we may not easily forget the misfortunes of the past, but we do ourselves greater harm by clinging onto them and allowing those misfortunes to control or limit what the future holds for us**.

Rick Warren, in his book *The Purpose Driven Life,* rightly explained that *"many people are driven by guilt. They spend their entire lives running from regrets and hiding their shame. Guilt-driven people are manipulated by memories. They allow their past to control their future... We are products of our past but we don't have to be prisoners of it. God's purpose is not limited by your past... God specialises in giving people a fresh start".*

Dear reader, if you have been imprisoned by any situation in your past, be assured; you can deal with it with God's help. I trust that this truth will motivate you to release the pains and bitterness of yesterday. By doing so, you will place yourself in readiness to receive the blessings and opportunities God has all this while kept in stock for you to enjoy.

> *"Therefore, as God's chosen people, holy and dearly loved, clothe yourselves with compassion, kindness, humility, gentleness and patience. Bear with each other and forgive one another if any of you has a grievance against someone. Forgive as the Lord forgave you."*
> **(Col 3:12-13 NIV)**

CHAPTER 3

A CLASSIC EXAMPLE THAT COULD HAVE JUSTIFIED BITTERNESS

In scripture, the experiences of a young man called Joseph, who was one of the twelve sons of Jacob, have a lot to teach everyone who has endured deep hurts from others. There are several experiences in his life that ordinarily should have made him a very bitter person. Considering the misfortunes that resulted from such experiences, the manner in which Joseph handled the complexities of his situation, and how God vindicated him in the end have many lessons for us to learn from. Indeed, it is a classic example.

"This is the account of Jacob's family line. Joseph, a young man of seventeen, was tending the flocks with his brothers, the sons of Bilhah and the sons of Zilpah, his father's wives, and he brought their father a bad report about them. Now Israel loved Joseph more than any of his other sons, because he had been born to him in his old age; and he made an ornate robe for him. When his brothers saw that their father loved him more than any of

them, they hated him and could not speak a kind word to him. Joseph had a dream, and when he told it to his brothers, they hated him all the more. He said to them, "Listen to this dream I had: We were binding sheaves of grain out in the field when suddenly my sheaf rose and stood upright, while your sheaves gathered around mine and bowed down to it." His brothers said to him, "Do you intend to reign over us? Will you actually rule us?" And they hated him all the more because of his dream and what he had said. Then he had another dream, and he told it to his brothers. "Listen," he said, "I had another dream, and this time the sun and moon and eleven stars were bowing down to me." When he told his father as well as his brothers, his father rebuked him and said, "What is this dream you had? Will your mother and I and your brothers actually come and bow down to the ground before you?" His brothers were jealous of him, but his father kept the matter in mind."

(Gen 37: 2-11 NIV)

From the passage, we can identify at least three reasons why Joseph's brothers turned out to hate him as much as they did.

1. His father loved him more than all the others, because he was the son of his old age. As a result, he treated him preferentially.

2. He shared his dreams freely and innocently with the members of his family. The dreams pointed to God's future intentions for him.

3. He had chosen the pathway of righteousness and had grown up as a well behaved son. He could not excuse the evil conduct of his brothers; he would report them to their father.

On the part of his brothers, these factors were their justification for hating him. These reasons formed the basis of the great trouble Joseph was to suffer. However, upon careful consideration of the factors, one would realise that these were no wrongs to justify the severe pain and suffering he endured at the hands of his brothers. Looking at the situation from Joseph's perspective gives a different insight into what the young man went through.

1. He suffered as a result of the actions of others

Joseph's choice to live as a righteous man attracted God's favour. He most likely did not pray for God to bless him with the gift of dreams. It was God's choice. That is to say, it was not his doing; it was the doing of the Lord.

Secondly, he had no hand in his father Jacob loving him more than the others. **It was his father's mistake**. Let me seize this opportunity to sound a note of caution to parents and guardians. Showing love and affection equally to all your children or dependants will serve as a unifying force. It helps the children to love one another. On the other hand, preferring some of your dependants or children over others will only pitch them against each other. As a parent, you must remember that you will not always be available to defend the position of your preferred child.

Jacob had fallen in love with Rachel, the younger of two sisters. Contrary to what he would have wanted, he was forced by culture to marry both sisters. Though he loved Rachel, she could not conceive to bear him children. Rather, Leah, the older sister was blessed with many children. So when God blessed Rachel with the son Joseph in Jacob's old age, he could not contain his joy. Joseph was regarded as the precious child. To make matters worse, Rachel lost her life while giving birth to a second son, Benjamin. From that time on, Jacob's love for Rachel was unconsciously redirected towards her two sons. This obviously attracted the displeasure of the other siblings, who became very jealous of Joseph. Benjamin, being very young and innocent, most likely did not see much. Joseph, on the other hand, had to endure so much mistreatment from his own brothers, though he had no control over his father's emotions. As it were, he suffered, not for his own mistakes, but for the mistakes of others. Since he had no control over those situations, he could not have prevented them in any way. It hurts very much when one goes through hard times as a result of the wrongs or the failings of others.

I know of a fairly well to do family whose lives turned around for the worse when the father fell in love with a younger lady, while still married to his wife of many years. He ran off with this lady and neglected his own family. From then on, the wife and six children had to struggle for many years to provide very basic needs for themselves. Their situation became quite desperate. The mother was saddled with debts; she had to borrow from every imaginable source to keep the family going. The boys were exposed to all kinds of dangers as they went away from home in efforts to make a living for themselves. One of the daughters, in an attempt to secure desperately needed financial support, ended up in a relationship she was not ready for. As you would imagine, everyone was very hurt by the father's actions. The entire family blamed him for all the struggles they had to endure as a result of his indiscretion. Some of the children, in later years, exhibited clearly intense feelings of bitterness towards their Dad.

Someone reading this book may have had similar experiences. As a result of divorce or remarriage of parents, some children lost the love, care or even the education they had been enjoying. Others ended up with step parents who made them feel like strangers in their own homes. There are people who have experienced prison life not because of wrongs they themselves committed; someone accused them falsely. Such innocent individuals could live with bitter feelings towards the people whose actions made them suffer, or blame them for lost opportunities in their lives. It takes great effort for a victim of circumstances of similar magnitude to handle such situations differently. This is why Joseph is such a great example.

2. He was hurt by those he loved and cared very much for

Experience has taught me that it is easier to deal with mistreatment, abuse or insults from someone who does not know who you are, your status, position or values. Relatively, dealing with the pain caused by someone who is expected to love and respect you is much more challenging. In other words, it hurts deeper when a loved one stabs you in the back. So when Joseph's love and affection for his brothers was reciprocated with such cruelty, it must have sent such sharp pains through his heart.

> *Now his brothers had gone to graze their father's flocks near Shechem, and Israel said to Joseph, "As you know, your brothers are grazing the flocks near Shechem. Come, I am going to send you to them." "**Very well**," he replied. So he said to him, "Go and see if*

all is well with your brothers and with the flocks, and bring word back to me." Then he sent him off from the Valley of Hebron. When Joseph arrived at Shechem, **a man found him wandering around in the fields** *and asked him, "What are you looking for?" He replied,* **"I'm looking for my brothers. Can you tell me where they are** *grazing their flocks?"* **"They have moved on from here,"** *the man answered. "I heard them say, 'Let's go to Dothan.'"* **So Joseph went after his brothers and found them near Dothan.**
(Genesis 37:12-17 NIV)

It is quite apparent from the passage that Joseph did not hesitate when he had the opportunity to follow his brothers to replenish them with fresh supplies. His deep concern for their wellbeing was demonstrated in how he was found wandering through the fields, making desperate efforts to locate them. If he did not really care for them, he would have returned and convinced his father that he had done his best, but could not find them. Rather, when he learnt that they had gone further on to Dothan, he gladly continued to cover the additional distance of about 30 kilometres with eager expectation to be a blessing to them. Sadly, however, while he saw them from a distance and started running with outstretched arms to embrace them, they quickly conspired to destroy him. They took advantage of his vulnerability to betray his love and hurt him in a very deep manner.

But they saw him in the distance, and before he reached them, they plotted to kill him. "Here comes that dreamer!" they said to each other. "Come now, let's kill him and throw him into one of these cisterns and say that a ferocious animal devoured him. Then we'll see what comes of his dreams."When Reuben heard this, he tried to rescue him from their hands. "Let's not take his life," he said. "Don't shed any blood. Throw him into this cistern here in the desert, but don't lay a hand on him." Reuben said this to rescue him from them and take him back to his father. So when Joseph came to his brothers, they stripped him of his robe—the ornate robe he was wearing – and they took him and threw him into the cistern. The cistern was empty; there was no water in it. As they sat down to eat their meal, they looked up and saw a caravan of Ishmaelites coming from Gilead. Their camels were loaded with spices, balm and myrrh, and they were on their way to take them down to Egypt. Judah said to his brothers, "What will we gain if we kill our brother and cover up his blood? Come, let's sell him to the Ishmaelites and not lay our hands on him; after all, he is our brother, our own flesh and blood." His brothers agreed. So when the Midianite merchants came by, his

> *brothers pulled Joseph up out of the cistern*
> *and sold him for twenty shekels of silver to the*
> *Ishmaelites, who took him to Egypt.*
> **(Gen 37: 18-28 NIV)**

You will agree with me that this level of betrayal will be difficult to ignore. The stab was indeed felt very deeply in the heart of a faithful wife, when the husband she so much trusted betrayed her love. This was when the man, to whom she had committed her whole life, got involved with another woman who was very well known to them. Also a mother who had loved, sacrificed and cared for her only child through thick and thin was later on in life accused by the same son of being a witch. The hurt could not have been felt any deeper than it did. He had ended up accusing his loving Mum of being the cause of his difficulties in life, and as a result, had turned his back on her. When situations like these end up turning ones world upside down, it is very difficult to deal with it or live with it.

Some years ago, I had an opportunity to share some of the thoughts in this book with the men of Her Majesty's Prison Service Institution in a city in the United Kingdom, during a Sunday morning service. In an interactive session after the ministration, a stoutly built young man walked up to me with tears in his eyes. As we sat down to talk, he shared with me in confidence how he believed the message had saved him from an imminent return to prison. He was set to commit a more serious crime after his release from prison. He explained how he had lived with a young lady whom he loved very dearly and was planning to marry. He, however, admitted doing something wrong that led to his incarceration for some months. While in custody, he had learnt that soon after his imprisonment, his best friend started going out with his fiancée. The lady had since moved in with his friend and had stopped visiting him in prison. While he told me his story, I felt the pain in those eyes looking straight into mine. The pain of being so deeply hurt by the two most important people in his life, and at a time when he needed their support the most, was unbearable. I therefore took the time to counsel him and prayed with him. Finally, he got up with the assurance that it had all happened for his own good. When I saw his readiness to forgive them and release them out of his life, in order to focus on his new found faith, I felt a great sense of fulfilment.

Turning our attention to the young man Joseph, can you imagine just how he must have felt when his outstretched arms of love were grabbed and twisted behind him before being thrown violently down an empty cistern? I can imagine the deep sorrow and bewilderment, as he wondered what his brothers were up to and what he had done to deserve this frightening reception. He certainly must have heard Judah saying, *"What would we gain if we kill him"*. And he must have gasped, "Oh my God! So they had even conspired together to kill me..." To confess, my eyes were filled with tears when I first reflected on the reality of what the young man must have gone through. It's generally hard to deal with hurts, but this level of betrayal of trust; from such close relations, must have been quite heavy on the tender heart of that innocent young man.

Eventually, they sold him into slavery. In later years, when his brothers realised the repercussions of their actions, they gave an indication of how Joseph had pleaded for them to have mercy on him. Recounting the time it had become obvious to Joseph that they were truly giving him away forever, they confessed among themselves: *"We saw how distressed he was when he pleaded with us for his life, but we would not listen" (Gen 42: 21).* It is quite possible that the cruelty they exhibited on that occasion never left his memory as he endured many years of suffering as a slave, with no rights in a foreign land.

3. He suffered for a very long time

Another reason why Joseph could have chosen to remain gloomy and bitter for the rest of his life was that, as a direct result of how his brothers dealt with him, he suffered for such a long time. The 39th and 40th chapters of the book of Genesis presents a depressing picture of how this young man's condition deteriorated from bad to worse, even while he made the effort to remain faithful to his God.

In Egypt, he was resold to Potiphar, who was a captain of Pharaoh's guards. During the period he was serving in his house, Potiphar's wife noticed his good looks and set a trap for him to have an affair with her. But being a God fearing man, he refused. This landed him in even bigger trouble. He was accused of attempted rape of his master's wife. As you would imagine, he was sent immediately into prison without trial and was completely forgotten by the outside world. While in jail, he met two people who used to serve in the palace. God used him to interpret important dreams they had while they were with him in prison. For one of them, his dream implied that he was soon to be released to go back and serve the king. While interpreting his dream, Joseph gave an indication of how he felt about his own situation as he pleaded; *"But when all goes well with you, remember me and show me kindness; mention me to Pharaoh and get me out of this prison. I was forcibly carried off from the land of the Hebrews, and even here I have done nothing to deserve being put in a dungeon" (Gen 40:14-15 NIV).*

Surprisingly, the moment that man gained his freedom and stepped out of the prison yard, he completely forgot about him. For two full years, he never once remembered that there was someone called Joseph who was wallowing in sorrow down there in the dungeon. I can only imagine how he must have felt at that lowest point in his life. Having been repeatedly rejected and disappointed by those he thought he could depend on, and with the future looking so gloomy and uncertain, I suppose he must have lost every shred of hope. Worst of all, the God, to whom he had been so loyal and faithful and for whose sake he had ended up in prison; by refusing to sin against him, also seemed to have abandoned him to his fate.

Dear reader, may I draw your attention to this fact that Joseph was 17 years of age when he had troubles with his brothers; which resulted in his misfortunes. He was 30 years old when he was brought out of prison to stand before Pharaoh on the day God vindicated him. This means that he had been through about 13 years of struggles as a result of how his brothers treated him. Regardless of these facts, when Joseph was later presented with the choice; to either get revenge or forgive his brothers for all they had done to him, he chose to forgive them.

> *"You have heard that it was said, 'Love your neighbor and hate your enemy.' But I tell you: Love your enemies and pray for those who persecute you, that you may be sons of your Father in heaven"*
> **(Matt 5: 43-45a NIV).**

CHAPTER 4

THE FORGIVENESS PATHWAY: JOSEPH'S OPTION

Unknown to Joseph, God was keeping him for a particular assignment, which was set for an appointed time. When God's set time was due, He came through for Joseph in a grand style. The occurrences that transformed his circumstances from an extended period of darkness into what his God had kept for him are explained in Genesis 41. Within a period of just one day; in fact within a matter of hours, God lifted Joseph from the position of a forgotten prisoner to become what I may refer to as the first Prime Minister of the entire nation of Egypt. Did I say Egypt? YES! Egypt – the very land into which he had been sold as a slave. Wow! What an awesome God we serve. Pharaoh had seen some disturbing dreams that night, which none of the wise men in the land could interpret. It was at that point that the servant, who used to be in the prison with Joseph, remembered him. He was reminded of a dream Joseph had interpreted for him while in prison, and he mentioned him to Pharaoh. What followed always bring tears in my eyes whenever I read this passage.

> *"So Pharaoh sent for Joseph, and he was*
> *quickly brought from the dungeon. When he*
> *had shaved and changed his clothes, he came*
> *before Pharaoh"*
> **(Gen 41:14 NIV).**

Pharaoh then went on to narrate his dreams. Joseph, by God's grace explained that the dream signified an imminent period of terrible hunger, which would last for seven years. This was, however, to be preceded by seven years of abundance of food. He then went ahead to advise the king to institute an action plan to save the nation. He advised Pharaoh to appoint a discreet and wise man to constitute a team, who will buy and store a fifth of the food that would be produced during the period of abundance. This would ensure that there was enough food for the nation during the period of hunger. Without hesitation Pharaoh asked his servants;

> *"...Can we find anyone like this man, one in*
> *whom is the spirit of God?" Then Pharaoh*
> *said to Joseph, "Since God has made all this*
> *known to you, there is no one so discerning*
> *and wise as you. You shall be in charge of my*
> *palace, and all my people are to submit to your*
> *orders. Only with respect to the throne will I be*
> *greater than you." So Pharaoh said to Joseph,*
> *"I hereby put you in charge of the whole land*

of Egypt." Then Pharaoh took his signet ring from his finger and put it on Joseph's finger. He dressed him in robes of fine linen and put a gold chain around his neck. He had him ride in a chariot as his second-in-command, and men shouted before him, "Make way!" Thus he put him in charge of the whole land of Egypt. Then Pharaoh said to Joseph, "I am Pharaoh, but without your word no one will lift hand or foot in all Egypt."
(Gen 41: 38-44 NIV)

Wow! Wow!! Wow!!! Indeed, weeping for the believer may endure for a night; but joy comes in the morning. What an awesome God we serve. The day had begun as gloomy as it had always been for many years. Suddenly, things turned around in such an ecstatic manner. This indeed could only be by the doing of the Lord.

Joseph soon forgot all his struggles. God blessed him with a beautiful wife and two lovely boys. He named them **Manasseh**: *"For God, said he, hath made me forget all my toil and all my father's house"*; and **Ephraim**: *"For God hath caused me to be fruitful in the land of my affliction"*. The meanings of these names themselves give further indication of the hurt and pain Joseph had carried in his heart through those very difficult periods of his life.

Soon, the period of abundance was over. As predicted, Egypt and the surrounding nations were stricken by unprecedented levels of food crisis. The situation reached epidemic proportions in the second year. This forced the silos to be opened for grains to be sold to the people of Egypt, under the able management of Joseph. By this time, Joseph was the second in command in the land. He had also become a very powerful man in the whole region. The hunger also hit his family in the land of Canaan. When his father Jacob heard that there was food in Egypt, he sent ten of Joseph's brothers to go and buy some corn for the family.

"When Jacob learned that there was grain in Egypt, he said to his sons, "Why do you just keep looking at each other?" He continued, "I have heard that there is grain in Egypt. Go down there and buy some for us, so that we may live and not die." Then ten of Joseph's brothers went down to buy grain from Egypt - - - So Israel's sons were among those who went to buy grain, for the famine was in the land of Canaan also. Now Joseph was the governor of the land, the person who sold grain to all its people. So when Joseph's brothers arrived, they bowed down to him with their faces to the ground. As soon as Joseph saw his brothers, he recognized them - - - Although Joseph recognized his brothers, they

did not recognize him. **Then he remembered his dreams about them - - -".**
(Gen 42:1-9 NIV)

On one usually busy day, Joseph was unexpectedly confronted with this situation that would awaken the emotions of any normal human being. With shock and confused emotions, Joseph saw his own brothers coming through the gates towards his throne to solicit for his help. He immediately recognised them, which suggests to me that there had been apparent lack of improvement in their lives. They on the other hand, could not recognise him. Obviously, God had so much elevated Joseph above their wildest imaginations.

It was on that fateful day, as they bowed before him, that Joseph remembered what the Lord had revealed to him over a decade earlier in his dreams. Permit me to use this premise to declare this fact to you, my dear reader. If only you will remain faithful to God, as the Lord unfolds his plan for your life in due course, you will surely remember everything he had said concerning you. None of His promises will fail.

In relating this situation to our lives, there is a big question that I would like you to honestly consider at this point. **Were you to be in Joseph's position, how would you have handled this situation?**

You would agree with me that should you be confronted with a situation of similar magnitude, you would most likely struggle in deciding which of these two possible pathways to take – *revenge* or *forgiveness.* Joseph's brothers committed very grievous crimes against him. The devastating consequences he had endured could have built deep resentment in his heart against them. And here he was, with the people who perpetrated such heinous crimes against him. They were in such vulnerable state and at his mercy and under his total control. There is an adage in my local dialect that says 'you do not sharpen the ends of branches which can damage your eyes; you rather cut them off completely and destroy them.' Most people would have considered this a God ordained time for sweet revenge. However, on this momentous occasion, Joseph decided to choose the more difficult option of forgiveness.

*"Then Joseph could no longer control himself before all his attendants, and he cried out, "Have everyone leave my presence!" So there was no one with Joseph when he made himself known to his brothers. And he wept so loudly that the Egyptians heard him, and Pharaoh's household heard about it. Joseph said to his brothers, "I am Joseph! Is my father still living?" But his brothers were not able to answer him, because they were terrified at his presence. **Then Joseph said to his brothers,***

"Come close to me." When they had done so, he said, "I am your brother Joseph, the one you sold into Egypt! And now, do not be distressed and do not be angry with yourselves for selling me here, because it was to save lives that God sent me ahead of you. *For two years now there has been famine in the land, and for the next five years there will not be plowing and reaping.* **But God sent me ahead of you to preserve for you a remnant on earth and to save your lives by a great deliverance. "So then, it was not you who sent me here, but God.** *He made me father to Pharaoh, lord of his entire household and ruler of all Egypt. Now hurry back to my father and say to him, 'This is what your son Joseph says: God has made me lord of all Egypt. Come down to me; don't delay.* **You shall live in the region of Goshen and be near me—you, your children and grandchildren, your flocks and herds, and all you have. I will provide for you there,** *because five years of famine are still to come.* **Otherwise you and your household and all who belong to you will become destitute.** *"You can see for yourselves, and so can my brother Benjamin, that it is really I who am speaking to you. Tell my father about all the honor accorded me in Egypt and about everything you have*

seen. And bring my father down here quickly."
Then he threw his arms around his brother
Benjamin and wept, and Benjamin embraced
him, weeping. **And he kissed all his brothers**
and wept over them. Afterward his brothers
talked with him."
(Gen 45:1-15 NIV)

There are some great lessons we can learn from the manner in which this young man responded to this challenging situation. Firstly, in spite of all they did to him, **it was Joseph who initiated the process of forgiveness**. They did not ask him to forgive them before he did. Obviously they couldn't have done so at this stage because they did not even know that this great man on whom their survival, and indeed their very lives depended was the same person they had treated so cruelly. At that moment, he had the opportunity of a lifetime to go down the history lane to recount what they had done to him, and how it had affected him for over a decade. He could have justified whatever act of retribution he would have chosen to vent his resentment on them in sweet revenge for their cruelty. Surprisingly, did you notice that the only mention of what they did to him was when revealed; *'I am your brother Joseph, the one you sold into Egypt'*? This was only intended to confirm to them that he was indeed the person he claimed to be. What!!! Was this young man not a normal human being? Did he not have the emotions of a normal human being? Was that all he could say about the past, before zooming into an endless lecture on the wonderful plans he had for them? Shouldn't he have made them know how he felt about what they had done to him? How could he simply brush all those lengthy years of pain he had to endure as a result of their cruelty under the carpet just like that? Of course he was normal, and he had emotions just as we all do. At one point, it was recorded; *"Then Joseph could no longer control himself before all his attendants, - - - And he wept so loudly that the Egyptians heard him, and Pharaoh's household heard about it"*. It surely was an emotional encounter. He simply refused to allow his emotions to dictate what to do and how to go about it. If only they had recognised the effects of their actions, and admitted their wrongdoings; it would have been a little easier to deal with the situation. Or if they had apologised and pleaded to be forgiven, there would have been some basis to tamper justice with mercy. However, as we shall soon learn, even after opening his heart and arms to accept them in such magnanimous manner, they never saw the need to truly apologise for what they did to him. Yet he did not at any point, treat them as the people who were responsible for the evils he suffered for so many years. He had simply made a choice to take the pathway of forgiveness. I believe that this exceptional reaction stemmed from some deeply rooted convictions, which I would like to draw your attention to:

1. He saw the hand of God in everything that happened to him:

Joseph considered everything that happened to him as God's channel of choice to ensure that the entire family would have adequate provision of food and resources during those difficult years. He must have felt privileged to be chosen for such a noble task – *"**But God sent me ahead of you to preserve for you a remnant on earth and to save your lives by a great deliverance. So then, it was not you who sent me here, but God"**.* By looking at things this way, he gave himself a genuine reason not to begrudge his brothers for what happened to him.

In relating this to our own situations, a better understanding of Romans 8:28 could similarly help us to wholeheartedly release those who may have so deeply hurt us. It says *"And we know that all things work together for good to them that love God and are called according to his purpose"* (KJV). Our lives as believers are all about fulfilling divine purpose. And God can not be limited by any situation in bringing you there. It does not matter whether what happened to you was by God's own initiative or an act of the Devil. Neither does it matter if it was intended for good or for evil; God is able to use all circumstances in our lives to achieve His purpose. There are bitter and happy moments in life, and what this scripture is saying is that the good and the bad, the sweet and the bitter, the valley bottom and the mountain top experiences are all brought together as recipes for a perfectly finished product. For example, not all the ingredients in a tasty sauce are sweet. While some could be consumed and enjoyed as single products, others may be too spicy to consume. Others still may be considered too sour or bitter. However, when the individual ingredients are handed over to a skillful cook, he or she is able to put them together to produce a tasty meal; the end product that everyone is interested in.

It was because Joseph considered the events in his life from this perspective that he was able to deal with the hurts. He recognised that it was through their actions that God had so elevated him. You could consider any painful or bitter experiences that someone's actions have caused you to go through, either in the past or perhaps at this very moment as spicy, but necessary ingredients to make you into what God intends you to be.

2. *He maintained his thoughts on the good that came out of the situation*

Considering what God had been able to do in his life, regardless of what happened in the past; it would have been a waste of spiritual energy to hold on to the past in bitterness. At least there was something to be thankful to God for. He must have wondered; had it not been for what the Lord had accomplished through those circumstances and the position he had been placed as a result, how would the family and the whole region have survived these terrible times? He chose to maintain his thoughts on the realisation that it was "*to preserve for you a remnant on earth and to save your lives by a great deliverance ... He made me father to Pharaoh, lord of his entire household and ruler of all Egypt*". Beloved, no matter how bitter your past or even present may be, there will always be something in your life to be grateful for.

I heard a story of a solo guitarist who, while performing before a large audience, had some of his guitar strings break one after another till he was left with three out of the normal six strings. The audience, realising what was happening, wandered whether he would bring the performance to a premature end. To their surprise, the solo artiste continued to make music with the remaining strings. With more pressure obviously exerted on them he soon lost two of the remaining, leaving a single string on the guitar. When at that stage the artiste carried on making some music from the single string, the crowd was moved to its feet in great amazement, giving him a thunderous applause. When he was later asked how he did it in spite of the unexpected disruption, he explained that many others would have allowed the loss to distract them, but **he chose to focus on what was left to make music with**. Similarly, we may rightly be reminded that life is more fulfilling when we allow ourselves to be propelled by what remains to make music with. Every attention given to what is lost will disorganise or disorient you and destroy the fun in your life. You have the choice to either major on the bad things happening in your life and stay down, or consciously pick out the good, no matter how insignificant they may seem to you, and allow them to give you reason to be grateful for your life.

One question that we cannot ignore, however, is whether Joseph would have treated his brothers with such dignity if he was still a prisoner or a devastated slave when he met them? In other words, how easy is it for a victim of the evils of others to forgive in similar manner, while the person is still at a low point in life, and still bearing the marks of the pain, or when there seems to be no good to focus on? Honestly, I cannot tell how he would have faced the challenge under such circumstances. However, there are several other examples, which give insight into how God would like us to deal with such situations.

The standard example is that of our Lord Jesus Christ himself *"For the joy set before him he endured the cross, scorning its shame ... Consider him who endured such opposition from sinners, so that you will not grow weary and lose heart" (Heb 12: 2, 3 NIV).* Regarding this, we are admonished to look onto him as the perfect example of our faith. While still on the cross, being taunted and mocked by his executioners and denied water when he desperately needed a sip, he was asking the father to forgive them. Jesus knew that whatever he was going through at that moment would work out for good as explained earlier. Indeed Joseph would not have known in prison that what he was going through was only a pathway to the next level in God's agenda for him. Knowing now from his example that God was indeed preparing him for a great future, we can base our admonition on his experiences. Though it would apparently have been more difficult if his brothers had come to him while still in prison, forgiveness would still have been the best option. Since you cannot tell what God can bring out of your situation, it is best to keep your heart free from bitterness and unforgiveness, even if you are still down. It will speed up the process of God's vindication when His time is due.

Should the example of Jesus be considered too high a standard, we may consider Stephen, who also chose to follow the example of Jesus. While he was being stoned to death for simply declaring the word of God, he cried out to God *"do not hold this sin against them"* before he died from their attack. You may be asking at this stage "how could I even consider a reason to forgive, while the abuses are still going on?" Yes, that may be a legitimate question to ask, but in order not to delay the good that the Lord is working out for you, the forgiveness option is still the best option.

3. He chose to overcome evil with good

Having said all these, some readers may still justify the grounds to remain bitter against those who have committed evils against them. It may not be apparent how God could under any circumstance, bring anything good out of their situation. Should this be your stand, let's yet consider another strong personal conviction, which must have influenced Joseph's decision to choose forgiveness rather than revenge. Joseph was a God fearing chap; this young man respected God and His word. If not for any reason at all, just because it was God's instruction to forgive, he would have done so. Under the New Covenant, we have even stronger admonition to choose forgiveness over revenge.

"Do not repay anyone evil for evil. **Be careful** *to do what is right in the eyes of everyone. If it is possible,* **as far as it depends on you***, live at peace with everyone. Do not take revenge, my dear friends, but leave room for God's wrath, for it is written: "It is mine to avenge; I will repay," says the Lord. On the contrary: "If your enemy is hungry, feed him; if he is thirsty, give him something to drink. In doing this, you will heap burning coals on his head."* **Do not be overcome by evil, but overcome evil with good.***"*
(Rom 12: 17-21 NIV)

This passage is quite instructive. Being admonished to *"**Be careful** to do what is right"* implies that it may not always be easy to forgive the wrongs others commit against you. This may be more so because even when you have decided to let go of your hurt, an offender could make it difficult for you to pursue that right pathway. For instance, it is much more difficult to let go of the hurt caused by an arrogant, unrepentant offender, or a persistent offender who takes your forgiveness for granted. In spite of that reality, we are admonished that "*if it is possible, **as far as it depends on you**, live at peace with everyone*". Hmm! Is it really possible to live at peace with EVERYONE? Careful thoughts on this scripture reveal, however, that the emphasis really is not on whether that is possible or not; it is a command for the child of God to obey. God requires the believer to take the position of a peacemaker, by doing whatever it takes on our part to ensure peace. It means that our forgiveness should not be conditional. We should not expect any input or reciprocal gesture from the offender before we commit ourselves to forgive. This is particularly so if you are dealing with someone who does not even know the Lord or who is not committed to living by the principles of Scripture. A careful study of the life of Joseph from Genesis chapters 37 to 50 reveals that his brothers never really apologised for what they did to him till after the death of their father. At that point, it became apparent that his brothers had thought that it was all because of their father that Joseph had received them. They simply could not believe that any normal person could just let such heinous crimes go unpunished. They therefore hatched a lie and sent a message to Joseph that their father had left a verbal will, instructing him not to hold their sins against them.

> *"When Joseph's brothers saw that their father was dead, they said, "What if Joseph holds a grudge against us and pays us back for all the wrongs we did to him?" So they sent word to Joseph, saying, "Your father left these instructions before he died: 'This is what you are to say to Joseph: I ask you to forgive your brothers the sins and the wrongs they committed in treating you so badly.' Now please forgive the sins of the servants of the God of your father." When their message came to him, Joseph wept."*
> **(Gen 50: 15-17 NIV)**

Why did Joseph weep on hearing this message? Because he could not understand why they had still not accepted the fact that he had truly and unconditionally forgiven them. He then called them and reassured them in these words; *"Don't be afraid. Am I in the place of God? You intended to harm me, but God intended it for good to accomplish what is now being done, the saving of many lives. So then don't be afraid, I will provide for you and your children"* (Gen 50: 19-21 NIV). This clearly demonstrates that without their input, the young man was able to completely release them from his heart, and received them with no trace of bitterness. Dearly beloved, so much, if not all, depends on us who are the true sons of the heavenly Father to let peace prevail (Matt 5:45a). Remember again that taking a stand for peace is not a sign of cowardice but a mark of maturity as a son of God; *"blessed are the peacemakers! For they shall be called the sons of God"* (Matt 5:9 MKJV).

Finally, though the passage acknowledges that some offenders, by virtue of their attitude may rightly deserve revenge, God reserves that right for Himself. *Do not repay anyone evil for evil ... Do not take revenge, my friends, but leave room for God's wrath, for it is written: "It is mine to avenge; I will repay," says the Lord.* He is such a caring God who knows everything you've been through. He defends the cause of the helpless and the innocent. Where vengeance is required, He promises to execute it; He does it in His own way and in His own time. Never should we therefore take it upon ourselves to avenge the wrongs that others commit against us.

It is quite apparent that Joseph had these convictions well settled in his heart before he was confronted with this difficult challenge. That explains a lot about his ability to overcome evil with good. It was the same kind of conviction that made David spare Saul's life when he found him fast asleep from exhaustion, after Saul had pursued David to kill him. He clearly understood these principles as indicated here:

"After Saul ... was told, "David is in the Desert of En Gedi. So Saul took three thousand able young men from all Israel and set out to look for David and his men ... a cave was there, and Saul went in to relieve himself. David and his men were far back in the cave. The men said, "This is the day the LORD spoke of when he said to you, 'I will give your enemy into your hands for you to deal with as you wish.'
*"Then David crept up unnoticed and cut off a corner of Saul's robe ... He said to his men, "The LORD forbid that I should do such a thing to my master, the LORD's anointed, or lay my hand on him; for he is the anointed of the LORD." With these words David rebuked his men and did not allow them to attack Saul. And Saul left the cave and went his way. Then David went out of the cave and called out to Saul, "My lord the king!" When Saul looked behind him, David bowed down and prostrated himself with his face to the ground. He said to Saul ... This day you have seen with your own eyes how the LORD delivered you into my hands in the cave. **Some urged me to kill you, but I spared you;** ... May the LORD judge between you and me. And **may the LORD avenge the wrongs you have done to me, <u>but my hand will not touch you</u>** ... May the LORD be our judge and decide between*

> *us. May he consider my cause and uphold it;*
> *may he vindicate me by delivering me from*
> *your hand."*
> **(1Sam 24:1-15 NIV)**

This is indeed unimaginable to the natural man. The sections I have emphasised reveal deep seated convictions that prevented David from avenging himself. And as our main passage in this section (Rom 12:17-21) indicates, whenever a child of God demonstrates this level of godly nature, it heaps *coals of fire,* or brings conviction upon even the most stubborn offender. This level of mature handling of hurts has the power to convert the naturally inconvertible. Child of God, would you rather win a soul for the kingdom, or push people away from the kingdom as a result of your unforgiving attitude? Consider the effect of David's actions on his pursuer:

> *"When David finished saying this, Saul asked,*
> *"Is that your voice, David my son?" And* ***he***
> ***wept aloud.*** ***"You are more righteous than I,"***
> *he said. "You have treated me well, but I have*
> *treated you badly. You have just now told me*
> *of the good you did to me; the LORD delivered*
> *me into your hands, but you did not kill me.*
> ***When a man finds his enemy, does he let him***
> ***get away unharmed? May the LORD reward***
> ***you well for the way you treated me today.*** ***I***

__know that you will surely be king and that the kingdom of Israel will be established in your hands__."
(1Sam 24:16-20 NIV)

That day, Saul realised that he could not destroy David, because the Lord must be with him to do what he had just done. David's reaction made so much difference in Saul's perception of who a true man of God is. And measuring it by his actions, he found himself not qualified to remain the King of Israel. If we are going to be able to meet the standard the Master requires of us, we must indeed build these biblical convictions deep into our being, to keep our hearts free from bitterness. Remember, dear reader, that there are two pathways to dealing with any kind of hurt. It's either the way of anger, bitterness and revenge on one hand, or the pathway of forgiveness. The latter requires a lot of sacrifice and maturity. Which way would you choose?

> *"Do not repay anyone evil for evil. Be careful to do what is right in the eyes of everyone. If it is possible, as far as it depends on you, live at peace with everyone. Do not be overcome by evil, but overcome evil with good"*
> **(Rom 12: 17, 18, and 21 NIV)**.

CHAPTER 5

NOW THAT YOU KNOW THESE THINGS WHAT WILL YOU DO?

My commitment to write this book was fuelled by a deep concern to help people avoid treading on the pathway of bitterness, which inevitably takes one through a life of misery and into a destination of doom. Before his death, Moses, a man who had a strong desire for his people to enjoy the fullness of God's blessings throughout their lifetime, cautioned his people accordingly: *"This day I call heaven and earth as witnesses against you that I have set before you life and death, blessings and curses. Now choose life, so that you and your children may live" (Deut 30: 19 NIV).* If you truly desire a life of peace and fulfilment, then you really do not have any choice other than to pursue the pathway of forgiveness. Jesus also said *"Now that you know these things, you will be blessed if you do them" (John 13:17 NIV).* Indeed if you reverence God and respect his instructions, you can not continue on the paths of bitterness and vengeance. You can make a commitment to overcome evil with good. Quite a while ago, I watched a talk show hosted by the renowned American philanthropist, Oprah Winfrey. In that episode, she interviewed a woman whose husband had stabbed their two twin daughters to death. An earlier interview with the husband, who was by then serving two consecutive life sentences in prison for the crimes, was also aired. The man was said to have been suffering from depression. The father had stabbed each of the twins more than a dozen times during a hide and seek playtime in their own home, while the wife was out. He then called 911 about 15 minutes later to report the incident to the Police. During the interview, the audience were shocked to learn that the woman had been paying regular visits to the man in prison and still considered him as her husband. She was carrying on with her life in the very house where her twin daughters were brutally murdered. The part that touched me most, as I watched the show, was when she indicated quite convincingly that she had genuinely forgiven her husband for what he had done. The show was so emotional that the usual applause, which is normally associated with the programme, was conspicuously absent. When pressed to explain how she could make such an unusual choice after such a terrible experience, she explained that the world feels that her husband does not deserve to live, because they are simply looking at a heartless father who has murdered his own daughters. She, however, was looking at a man who in an instant was overwhelmed by a bout of depression, which resulted in a tragic end. The second powerful statement she made was that while the world was interested in the most deserving punishment for the man, she was considering how people like her husband could be helped to prevent them from ending up the way he did. She indicated her commitment to deal with her pain in order to be in good shape to provide that needed support to the same man who had caused her such much pain. Though she admitted, she was most likely going to live with the pain for the rest of her life.

I was so touched by the choice the woman had made and felt the urge to pray for her at that very moment for grace to fulfil her commitment. This woman's response to this tragic incident reaffirms the point I am making here that you can make a choice to overcome evil with good. It all depends on the angle from which you consider the issues involved. If you choose to go along the pathway of revenge, you will certainly find the justification for your choice. In the same way, if you decide to go the way our Lord Jesus taught us, you will find strength in Him to see it through.

Dear reader, if you have been touched in any way by the thoughts shared in this book and you wish to do something about your pain, then the best time to do it is _**NOW**_. Do not wait any longer, because the Devil, who wants to keep you where you don't belong, has not stopped working on you. Taking the initiative towards forgiveness may be quite simple for some people. For many others, it is certainly going to be a huge struggle, regardless of the convictions the Holy Spirit may impress on their hearts. There is going to be a struggle between hanging on to your emotions of pain and obeying the voice of the Spirit to release those who have caused you the pain. **Emotions, whether positive or negative, are powerful. Regardless, we should not allow**

them to determine the choices we make in life. Emotions are usually temporal, and we should not make decisions that will affect us permanently on the basis of how we feel now. The question we should ask ourselves is whether there is any satisfaction in clogging our hearts with the pain of bitterness. If there is any satisfaction at all, the benefit of freeing your heart through forgiveness far outweighs it. Make a commitment to overcome evil with good.

Making the choice to obey the promptings of the Holy Spirit is the most important step, because no one can make that decision for you. Once you have made that decision, you can then be helped all the way through. Once you have made the decision to pursue forgiveness, the following steps will be of great help in achieving the desired results.

1. First seek God's help in prayer

"For it is God which worketh in you both to WILL and to DO of his good pleasure" (Phil 2:13 *KJV*). We are admonished to "approach the throne of grace". If God has brought you this far, where you are considering forgiving what you never thought you could, it means He has made you *willing* to deal with it the right way. Through earnest prayer for His help, He will also make you *able to do* it. You do not have to be worried about your hesitation to take the initiative, because God is fully aware of your weaknesses. That is the more reason why we should look up to Him for help.

Be assured, the Lord will not condemn your hesitation; He is rather standing by to help you overcome it. He has been where you are now and so He understands. When Jesus was overwhelmed with deep sorrow at the point of his death, he hesitated and asked the Father to let the cup pass over him if it were possible. However, because it was for that very reason that God made Him come, He simply had to yield. So today, as you struggle to yield to His call to forgive, He is right there with you as this scripture confirms: *"Our High Priest is not one who cannot feel sympathy for our weakness. On the contrary, we have a High Priest who was tempted in every way that we are, but did not sin. Let us have confidence, then, and approach God's throne, where there is grace. **There we will receive mercy and find grace to help us just when we need it"*** (Heb 4: 15-16 *GNB*). Now is the best time to seek this grace and mercy, which will help free your heart in readiness for what God has kept in store for you all this while; but which you had no space in your heart to receive.

2. Approach it with the right attitude

Before you do anything, permit me to draw your attention to the powerful effect of ***attitude***. The attitude with which you approach this difficult process will have a lot to do in determining where it all ends. If you go in with such an attitude of a perfect one who is being "pushed" by the Lord to show mercy to a worthless sinner who does not really deserve your forgiveness, the effort will achieve nothing. Your self righteous attitude will be evident and your effort will be rejected in a way which could cause you more pain. To help you overcome this hidden but real possibility, it will be helpful to admit your role in the whole incident and ask for God's forgiveness. Ask Him to forgive you for harbouring bitterness in your heart for this long before you ask for the grace to forgive others. The truth is, when you consider yourself as having contributed in bringing the issue this far, you will not go in with a self righteous attitude.

3. Take a practical action to initiate the forgiveness process

You may need to pick up the phone *now*, or write a note *now* and send it through *today,* to set the stage for any possible further discussions or meetings to sort things out. Following biblical guidelines (Matt 18: 15-17), it may be best to do it personally and alone, unless it is beyond you. Do not allow any initial obstacles or adamant attitude from the person you seek to forgive, stop you. You will need to persevere – *as far as it depends on you* – till you gain your brother or sister fully in order to fulfil the admonishing to *live at peace with all men*. **This calls for great deal of humility.** You will have to lay down your pride and dignity and stoop very low, all for the sake of Christ. If you need to talk about the issues that caused you the pain, **please do**

not criticise or attack your offender. That will be counter-productive. The person will simply be defensive and hurt you the more. Rather than criticising, **talk about how you feel** regarding what happened. The point here is, when you talk about **your feelings** you are not talking about their actions per sé, but about how **you** took it. **So they do not feel attacked**, because it is not about how bad their actions were; it's about what it did to your feelings. It could well be that due to some personal experiences in your past, you always feel offended when someone does something to you in a particular way. In a situation like that, the offender is usually touched when he or she realises that their action, which may have had no adverse effect on others, did affect you negatively. In other words, while what they did may not have been adjudged as bad by others and may have meant nothing to them or to others, it did hurt you. This approach would almost always draw apologies from the offender.

4. Press on till you achieve total reconciliation

After going through this personal review and evaluation, I would recommend that you do not end it all there. Go a step further and seek reconciliation. Forgiveness does not necessarily end in total reconciliation. Let me illustrate it: It's like two people walking along holding hands. If something comes between them physically, it could separate their hands from each other. The process of forgiveness, which I have explained is like the two coming into agreement to remove the obstacle that has come between them. Once that has been done, the two can choose to keep walking together, but without holding hands any longer. That is not reconciliation. Reconciliation takes place only when one of them stretches out a hand to the other partner to offer the opportunity to hold that arm again. Someone could say, "Well I have forgiven him or her but I will have to keep my distance." I must admit that under some circumstances e.g. in simple job related relationships with colleagues at a work place, it may be a wise thing to do to prevent further hurts. However, in more binding relationships such as sibling or marriage, you will need to do everything possible to seek total reconciliation, in order to derive the full benefit of forgiveness.

After talking things over, reconciliation becomes easier if you are able to submit yourself to a friendly or loving gesture such as a hand shake, a hug or a kiss, depending on the level of relationship between you and your offender. Do not wait for it to come from the other party; eagerly offer the gesture to signify how truly you have released the person from your heart.

My dear reader, I would like to finally remind you that God took the initiative for our forgiveness and we should follow that example. It is my prayer that as you seek to follow His example, the good Lord would work on you to *will* and to *do* of His good pleasure. God richly bless you.

Lightning Source UK Ltd.
Milton Keynes UK
UKOW02f0624311014

240863UK00002B/233/P